STIMULATING MESSAGES FROM SWAMI VIVEKANANDA (2ND ED)

SELECTED FOR STUDENTS

COMPILATION - DR ASHOK BANERJI

In Tribute to

Swami Vivekananda

National Youth day

12th January 2023

Contents

Preface

This book is intended to introduce the profound messages of Swami Vivekananda to students. Swami Vivekananda was born on 12th January 1863, in Calcutta presently known as Kolkata, India. He left his mortal body on 4th July 1902. His Birthday is celebrated as National Youth Day in India.

It is indeed difficult to narrate his contributions in a few words. In him, we can find a spiritual guide, revivalist of Sanatan Hinduism, patriot, philosopher and so many others. His arrival created a new life in India and the world at a juncture when materialism was eroding the ancient religious foundations.

He propagated the age-old wisdom of Vedas and Puranas in a new light in India and the West. His teachings and timeless message are a treasure for mankind. His words encourage, inspire and offer guidance for a purposeful life.

Fortunately, some of his teaching and thoughts could have been recorded during the last nine years of his life. It is published as the Complete Works of Swami Vivekananda by Advaita Asrama, a publication centre of Ramakrishna Mission since 1907. This 9-volume book is a goldmine of wisdom that electrifies readers of all ages.

However, the sheer volume and the variety of the issues discussed may become overwhelming for the students to start with. This selection is compiled precisely to overcome these challenges.

While teaching computers especially, computational thinking and coding to children I realised the importance of Swami Vivekananda's words - education "should not be for filling some facts into the brain. It should be for the preparation for life. It should be for "life-building, man-making, character-making, assimilation of ideas".

Swamiji suggested that education should be for reforming the minds. His messages are essential for every student. For this purpose, this booklet is prepared for students as a concise initial reading while they delve into the curricular subjects.

The selected stories, quotes and poems in the words of Swamaji would inspire and guide the young learners in their learning journey.

Words of the original writings have been maintained, only paragraph breaks have been added in some places to aid young readers.

Hopefully, this small book will inspire you to explore further and be a real human being.

Any suggestions are welcome.

Regards
Dr. Ashok Banerji
DrAshokBanerji@gmail.com

Online Resources
The Complete Works of Swami Vivekananda
https://advaitaashrama.org/cw/
Life of Swami Vivekananda
https://belurmath.org/swami-vivekananda/

CHAPTER ONE

Why we disagree

The story as narrated by Swami Vivekananda goes like this -*

I will tell you a little story. You have heard the eloquent speaker who has just finished say, "Let us cease from abusing each other," and he was very sorry that there should be always so much variance. But I think I should tell you a story which would illustrate the cause of this variance.

A frog lived in a well. It had lived there for a long time. It was born there and brought up there, and yet was a little, small frog.

Of course, the evolutionists were not there then to tell us whether the frog lost its eyes or not, but, for our story's sake, we must take it for granted that it had its eyes, and that it every day cleansed

the water of all the worms and bacilli that lived in it with an energy that would do credit to our modern bacteriologists. In this way, it went on and became a little sleek and fat.

Well, one day another frog that lived in the sea came and fell into the well.

"Where are you from?"

"I am from the sea."

"The sea! How big is that? Is it as big as my well?" and he took a leap from one side of the well to the other.

"My friend," said the frog of the sea, "how do you compare the sea with your little well?"

Then the frog took another leap and asked, "Is your sea so big?"

"What nonsense you speak, to compare the sea with your well!"

"Well, then," said the frog of the well, "nothing can be bigger than my well; there can be nothing bigger than this; this fellow is a liar, so turn him out."

That has been the difficulty all the while.

Swamiji concludes:

... I am sitting in my own little well and thinking that the whole world is my little well. ... break down the barriers of this little world of ours, and hope that, in the future, the Lord will help you to accomplish your purpose.

*(Complete Works of Swami Vivekananda, V.1: At the Parliament of Religion, Why we disagree, p4-5)

TO THE FOURTH OF JULY
Behold, the dark clouds melt away,
That gathered thick at night, and hung
So like a gloomy pall above the earth!
Before thy magic touch, the world
Awakes. The birds in chorus sing.
The flowers raise their star-like crowns —
Dew-set, and wave thee welcome fair.
The lakes are opening wide in love
Their hundred thousand lotus-eyes
To welcome thee, with all their depth.
All hail to thee, thou Lord of Light!
A welcome new to thee, today,
O Sun! Today thou sheddest Liberty!

......

.....

Swami Vivekananda left his mortal body on the 4th of July, 1902. On the 4th of July, 1898, while travelling to Kashmir with some American disciples, he prepared this poem. Only 1st paragraph included here. (CW(5), Writings: Prose and Poems)

CHAPTER TWO

Discovery

This story as narrated by Swami Vivekananda goes like this -*

We say Newton discovered gravitation**. Was it sitting anywhere in a corner waiting for him? It was in his own mind; the time came and he found it out. All knowledge that the world has ever received comes from the mind; the infinite library of the universe is in your own mind.

The external world is simply the suggestion, the occasion, which sets you to study your own mind, but the object of your study is always your own mind.

The falling of an apple gave the suggestion to Newton, and he studied his own mind.

He rearranged all the previous links of thought in his mind and discovered a new link among them, which we call the law of gravitation. It was not in the apple nor in anything in the centre of the earth.

All knowledge, therefore, secular or spiritual, is in the human mind. In many cases, it is not discovered, but remains covered, and when the covering is being slowly taken off, we say, "We are learning," and the advance of knowledge is made by the advance of this process of uncovering.

Swamiji concludes:

The man from whom this veil is being lifted is the more knowing man, the man upon whom it lies thick is ignorant, and the man from whom it has entirely gone is all-knowing, omniscient.

There have been omniscient men, and, I believe, there will be yet; and that there will be myriads of them in the cycles to come.

*(Complete Works of Swami Vivekananda, V.1, Karma Yoga, Chapter 1, p28-29)

** *Evidence suggests that Indian mathematician/ astronomer Brahmagupta (c.598 – c.668 CE) first described gravity as an attractive force, using the term "gurutvākarṣaṇam (गुरुत्वाकर्षणम्)".*

THOU BLESSED DREAM

·

If things go ill or well —
If joy rebounding spreads the face,
Or sea of sorrow swells —
A play — we each have part,
Each one to weep or laugh as may;
Each one his dress to don —
Its scenes, alternative shine and rain.

·

Thou dream, O blessed dream!
Spread far and near thy veil of haze,
Tone down the lines so sharp,
Make smooth what roughness seems.

·

No magic but in thee!
Thy touch makes desert bloom to life.
Harsh thunder, sweetest song,
Fell death, the sweet release.

....

(Written to Miss Christine Greenstidel from Paris, 14th August 1900, CW(8), Writings: Poems)

CHAPTER THREE

Controlling the Mind

Swami Vivekananda's narration goes like this -*

How hard it is to control the mind! Well has it been compared to the maddened monkey.

There was a monkey, restless by his own nature, as all monkeys are. As if that were not enough someone made him drink freely of wine, so that he became still more restless.

Then a scorpion stung him. When a man is stung by a scorpion, he jumps about for a whole day; so, the poor monkey found his condition worse than ever.

To complete his misery a demon entered into him. What language can describe the uncontrollable restlessness of that monkey?

The human mind is like that monkey, incessantly active by its own nature; then it becomes drunk with the wine of desire, thus increasing its turbulence.

After desire takes possession comes the sting of the scorpion of jealousy at the success of others, and last of all the demon of pride enters the mind, making it think itself of all importance. How hard to control such a mind!

The first lesson, then, is to sit for some time and let the mind run on. The mind is bubbling up all the time. It is like that monkey jumping about. Let the monkey jump as much as he can; you simply wait and watch.

Knowledge is power, says the proverb, and that is true. Until you know what the mind is doing you cannot control it. Give it the rein; many hideous thoughts may come into it; you will be astonished that it was possible for you to think such thoughts. But you will find that each day the mind's vagaries are becoming less and less violent, that each day it is becoming calmer.

In the first few months you will find that the mind will have a great many thoughts, later you will find that they have somewhat decreased, and in a few more months they will be fewer and fewer, until at last the mind will be under perfect control; but we must patiently practice every day.

As soon as the steam is turned on, the engine must run; as soon as things are before us, we must perceive; so a man, to prove that he is not a machine, must demonstrate that he is under the control of nothing.

Swamiji concludes:

This controlling of the mind, and not allowing it to join itself to the centres, is Pratyahara. How is this practised? It is a tremendous work, not to be done in a day. Only after a patient, continuous struggle for years can we succeed.

*(Complete Works of Swami Vivekananda, Vol.1, Raja Yoga, Chapter IV, p174,175)

NIRVANASHATKAM, OR SIX STANZAS ON NIRVANA

.

I am neither the mind, nor the intellect, nor the ego,
nor the mind-stuff;
I am neither the body, nor the changes of the body;
I am neither the senses of hearing, taste, smell, or sight,
Nor am I the ether, the earth, the fire, the air;
I am Existence Absolute, Knowledge Absolute, Bliss
Absolute —
I am He, I am He. (Shivoham, Shivoham).

-

I am neither the Prâna, nor the five vital airs;
I am neither the materials of the body, nor the five
sheaths;
Neither am I the organs of action, nor object of the senses;
I am Existence Absolute, Knowledge Absolute, Bliss
Absolute —
I am He, I am He. (Shivoham, Shivoham).

....

.....

(part of Translation of a poem by Shankarâchârya. CW(4), Writings: Poems)

Escape of minister

This story as narrated by Swami Vivekananda goes like this -*

There was once a minister to a great king. He fell into disgrace. The king, as a punishment, ordered him to be shut up in the top of a very high tower. This was done, and the minister was left there to perish.

He had a faithful wife, however, who came to the tower at night and called to her husband at the top to know what she could do to help him. He told her to return to the tower the following night and bring with her a long rope, some stout twine, a pack of thread, silken thread, a beetle, and a little honey.

Wondering much, the good wife obeyed her husband and brought him the desired articles. The husband directed her to attach the silken thread firmly to the beetle, then to smear its horns with a drop of honey, and to set it free on the wall of the tower, with its head pointing upwards. She obeyed all these instructions, and the beetle started on its long journey.

Smelling the honey ahead it slowly crept onwards, in the hope of reaching the honey, until at last, it reached the top of the tower, when the minister grasped the beetle and got possession of the silken thread.

He told his wife to tie the other end to the pack thread, and after he had drawn up the pack thread, he repeated the process with the stout twine, and lastly with the rope.

Then the rest was easy. The minister descended from the tower by means of the rope, and made his escape.

Swamiji concludes:

In this body of ours, the breath motion is the "silken thread"; by laying hold of and learning to control it we grasp the pack thread of the nerve currents and from these the stout twine of our thoughts, and lastly the rope of Prana, controlling which we reach freedom.

*(Complete Works of Swami Vivekananda, Vol.1, Raja Yoga, chapter II, The First Steps, p 143-144)

Excerpts from Poetry NO ONE TO BLAME
(Written from New York, 16th May, 1895.)

-

The sun goes down, its crimson rays
Light up the dying day;
A startled glance I throw behind
And count my triumph shame;
No one but me to blame.

.....

I cast off fear and vain remorse,
I feel my Karma's sway
I face the ghosts my deeds have raised —
Joy, sorrow, censure, fame;
No one but me to blame.

Good, bad, love, hate, and pleasure, pain
Forever linked go,
I dream of pleasure without pain,
It never, never came;
No one but me to blame.

I give up hate, I give up love,
My thirst for life is gone;
Eternal death is what I want,
Nirvanam goes life's flame;
No one is left to blame.

......

...

(CW(8), Writings: Poems)

CHAPTER FIVE

Story of God & Demon

Swami Vivekananda's narration goes like this -

A god and a demon went to learn about the Self from a great sage. They studied with him for a long time. At last, the sage told them, "You yourselves are the Being you are seeking."

Both of them thought that their bodies were the Self. They went back to their people quite satisfied and said, "We have learned everything that was to be learned; eat, drink, and be merry; we are the Self; there is nothing beyond us."

The nature of the demon was ignorant, clouded; so he never inquired any further but was perfectly contented with the idea that he was God, that by the Self was meant the body.

The god had a purer nature. He at first committed the mistake of thinking: I, this body, am Brahman: so keep it strong and in health, and well dressed, and give it all sorts of enjoyments. But, in a few days, he found out that that could not be the meaning of the sage, their master; there must be something higher.

So, he came back and said, "Sir, did you teach me that this body was the Self? If so, I see all bodies die; the Self cannot die." The sage said, "Find it out; thou art That." Then the god thought that the vital forces which work the body were what the sage meant. But. after a time, he found that if he ate, these vital forces remained strong, but, if he starved, they became weak.

The god then went back to the sage and said, "Sir, do you mean that the vital forces are the Self ?" The sage said, "Find out for yourself; thou art That."

The god returned home once more, thinking that it was the mind, perhaps, that was the Self. But in a short while he saw that thoughts were so various, now good, again bad; the mind was too changeable to be the Self.

He went back to the sage and said, "Sir, I do not think that the mind is the Self; did you mean that?" "No," replied the sage, "thou art That; find out for yourself."

The god went home, and at last found that he was the Self, beyond all thought, one without birth or death, whom the sword cannot pierce or the fire burn, whom the air cannot dry or the water melt, the beginningless and endless, the immovable, the intangible, the omniscient, the omnipotent Being; that It was neither the body nor the mind, but beyond them all.

Swamiji concludes:

So he was satisfied; but the poor demon did not get the truth, owing to his fondness for the body.

*(Complete Works of Swami Vivekananda, Vol.1, Raja Yoga, chapter II, The First Steps, p 140-141)

THE CUP

.

This is your cup — the cup assigned
to you from the beginning.
Nay, My child, I know how much
of that dark drink is your own brew
Of fault and passion, ages long ago,
In the deep years of yesterday, I know.

.

This is your road — a painful road and drear.
I made the stones that never give you rest.
I set your friend in pleasant ways and clear,
And he shall come like you, unto My breast.
But you, My child, must travel here.

-

This is your task. It has no joy nor grace,
But it is not meant for any other hand,
And in My universe bath measured place,
Take it. I do not bid you understand.
I bid you close your eyes to see My face.

.....

(CW(6) Writings: Prose and Poems)

CHAPTER SIX

Oyster

This story as narrated by Swami Vivekananda goes like this -*

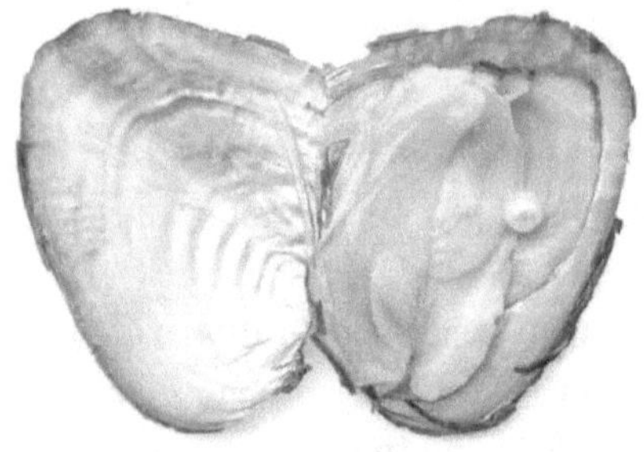

Be like the pearl oyster. There is a pretty Indian fable to the effect that if it rains when the star Svâti is in the ascendant, and a drop of rain falls into an oyster, that drop becomes a pearl.

The oysters know this, so they come to the surface when that star shines, and wait to catch the precious raindrop. When a drop falls into them, quickly the oysters close their shells and dive down to the bottom of the sea, there to patiently develop the drop into the pearl.

We should be like that. First hear, then understand, and then, leaving all distractions, shut your minds to outside influences, and devote yourselves to developing the truth within you.

There is the danger of frittering away your energies by taking up an idea only for its novelty and then giving it up for another that is newer. Take one thing up and do it, and see the end of it, and before you have seen the end, do not give it up.

Swamiji concludes:

He who can become mad with an idea, he alone sees light. Those that only take a nibble here and a nibble there will never attain anything. They may titillate their nerves for a moment, but there it will end. They will be slaves in the hands of nature, and will never get beyond the senses.

*(Complete Works of Swami Vivekananda, Vol.1, Raja yoga, Chapter IV, p177)

LIGHT

.

I look behind and after
And find that all is right,
In my deepest sorrows
There is a soul of light

.

.(From a letter toMiss MacLeod, 26th December 1900 (Vide Vol. VI.), CW(8), Writings: Poems)

Perseverance

This story as narrated by Swami Vivekananda goes like this* -

There was a great god-sage called Nârada. Just as there are sages among mankind, great Yogis, so there are great Yogis among the gods. Narada was a good Yogi, and very great. He travelled everywhere.

One day he was passing through a forest, and saw a man who had been meditating until the white ants had built a huge mound round his body — so long had he been sitting in that position.

He said to Narada, "Where are you going?" Narada replied, "I am going to heaven." "Then ask God when He will be merciful to me; when I shall attain freedom."

Further on Narada saw another man. He was jumping about, singing, dancing, and said, "Oh, Narada, where are you going?" His voice and his gestures were wild. Narada said, "I am going to heaven." "Then, ask when I shall be free." Narada went on.

In the course of time, he came again by the same road, and there was the man who had been meditating with the ant-hill round him.

He said, "Oh, Narada, did you ask the Lord about me?" "Oh, yes." "What did He say?" "The Lord told me that you would attain freedom in four more births."

Then the man began to weep and wail, and said, "I have meditated until an ant-hill has grown around me, and I have four more births yet!"

Narada went to the other man. "Did you ask my question?" "Oh, yes. Do you see this tamarind tree? I have to tell you that as many leaves as there are on that tree, so many times, you shall be born, and then you shall attain freedom."

The man began to dance for joy, and said, "I shall have freedom after such a short time!"

A voice came, "My child, you will have freedom this minute." That was the reward for his perseverance. He was ready to work through all those births, nothing discouraged him. But the first man felt that even four more births were too long.

Swamiji concludes:

Only perseverance, like that of the man who was willing to wait aeons brings about the highest result.

*(Complete Works of Swami Vivekananda, Vol.1, Raja Yoga, Chapter VIII, p193-194)

HOLD ON YET A WHILE, BRAVE HEART

.

If the sun by the cloud is hidden a bit,
If the welkin shows but gloom,
Still hold on yet a while, brave heart,
The victory is sure to come.

...

The duties of life are sore indeed,
And its pleasures fleeting, vain,
The goal so shadowy seems and dim,
Yet plod on through the dark, brave heart,
With all thy might and main.

.

Not a work will be lost, no struggle vain,
Though hopes be blighted, powers gone;
Of thy loins shall come the heirs to all,
Then hold on yet a while, brave soul,
No good is e'er undone.

....

(Written to H. H. The Maharaja of Khetri, Rajputana, CW(4), Writings: Poems)

CHAPTER EIGHT

Morality

The story as narrated by Swami Vivekananda goes like this*-

There was a certain king who had a huge number of courtiers, and each one of these courtiers declared he was ready to sacrifice his life for his master, and that he was the most sincere being ever born.

In course of time, a Sannyâsin came to the king. The king said to him that there never was a king who had so many sincere courtiers as he had. The Sannyasin smiled and said he did not believe that.

The king said the Sannyasin could test it if he liked. So, the Sannyasin declared that he would make a great sacrifice by which the king's reign would be extended very long, with the condition that there should be made a small tank into which each one of his courtiers should pour a pitcher of milk, in the dark of night.

The king smiled and said, "Is this the test?" And he asked his courtiers to come to him, and told them what was to be done. They all expressed their joyful assent to the proposal and returned.

In the dead of night, they came and emptied their pitchers into the tank. But in the morning, it was found full of water only. The courtiers were assembled and questioned about the matter. Each one of them had thought there would be so many pitchers of milk that his water would not be detected.

Swamiji concludes:

Unfortunately, most of us have the same idea and we do our share of work as did the courtiers in the story.

*(Complete Works of Swami Vivekananda, Vol.1, Vedanta and Privilege, p427-428)

Story of a Ghost

This story as narrated by Swami Vivekananda goes like this* -

There was a poor man who wanted some money; and somehow he had heard that if he could get hold of a ghost, he might command him to bring money or anything else he liked; so he was very anxious to get hold of a ghost.

He went about searching for a man who would give him a ghost, and at last, he found a sage with great powers and besought his help. The sage asked him what he would do with a ghost.

I want a ghost to work for me; teach me how to get hold of one, sir; I desire it very much," replied the man. But the sage said, "Don't disturb yourself, go home."

The next day the man went again to the sage and began to weep and pray, "Give me a ghost; I must have a ghost, sir, to help me."

At last, the sage was disgusted, and said, "Take this charm, repeat this magic word, and a ghost will come, and whatever you say to him he will do. But beware; they are terrible beings, and must be kept continually busy. If you fail to give him work, he will take your life."

The man replied, "That is easy; I can give him work for all his life." Then he went to a forest, and after long repetition of the magic word, a huge ghost appeared before him, and said, "I am a ghost. I have been conquered by your magic; but you must keep me constantly employed. The moment you fail to give me work I will kill you."

The man said, "Build me a palace," and the ghost said, "It is done; the palace is built."

"Bring me money," said the man. "Here is your money," said the ghost.

"Cut this forest down, and build a city in its place." "That is done," said the ghost, "anything more?"

Now the man began to be frightened and thought he could give him nothing more to do; he did everything in a trice.

The ghost said, "Give me something to do or I will eat you up."

The poor man could find no further occupation for him, and was frightened. So he ran and ran and at last reached the sage, and said, "Oh, sir, protect my life!"

The sage asked him what the matter was, and the man replied, "I have nothing to give the ghost to do. Everything I tell him to do he does in a moment, and he threatens to eat me up if I do not give him work."

Just then the ghost arrived, saying, "I'll eat you up," and he would have swallowed the man. The man began to shake, and begged the sage to save his life.

The sage said, "I will find you a way out. Look at that dog with a curly tail. Draw your sword quickly and cut the tail off and give it to the ghost to straighten out." The man cut off the dog's tail and gave it to the ghost, saying, "Straighten that out for me."

The ghost took it and slowly and carefully straightened it out, but as soon as he let it go, it instantly curled up again. Once more he laboriously straightened it out, only to find it again curled up as soon as he attempted to let go of it.

Again he patiently straightened it out, but as soon as he let it go, it curled up again. So he went on for days and days, until he was exhausted and said, "I was never in such trouble before in my life. I am an old veteran ghost, but never before was I in such trouble."

"I will make a compromise with you;" he said to the man, "you let me off and I will let you keep all I have given you and will promise not to harm you." The man was much pleased and acccpted the offer gladly.

Swamiji concludes:

This world is like a dog's curly tail, and people have been striving to straighten it out for hundreds of years; but when they let it go, it has curled up again.

(CW(1), Karma Yoga, Chapter V, WE HELP OURSELVES, NOT THE WORLD)

THE ATTAINMENT OF FREEDOM

....

....

Freedom is the motive of the universe, freedom its goal. The laws of nature are the methods through which we are struggling to reach that freedom, under the guidance of Mother. This universal struggle for freedom attains its highest expression in man in the conscious desire to be free. This freedom is attained by the threefold means of — work, worship, and knowledge.

(a) Work — constant, unceasing effort to help others and love others.
(b) Worship — consists in prayer, praise, and meditation.
(c) Knowledge — that follows meditation.

(CW(5), III. The Absolute and the Attainment of Freedom)

CHAPTER TEN

Lion in a flock of sheep

The story as narrated by Swami Vivekananda goes like this-

Shall we advise men to kneel down and cry, "O miserable sinners that we are!" No, rather let us remind them of their divine nature.

I will tell you a story. A lioness in search of prey came upon a flock of sheep, and as she jumped at one of them, she gave birth to a cub and died on the spot. The young lion was brought up in the flock, ate grass, and bleated like a sheep, and it never knew that it was a lion.

One day a lion came across the flock and was astonished to see in it a huge lion eating grass and bleating like a sheep. At his sight the flock fled and the lion-sheep with them.

But the lion watched his opportunity and one day found the lion-sheep asleep.

He woke him up and said, "You are a lion." The other said, "No," and began to bleat like a sheep. But the stranger lion took him to a lake and asked him to look in the water at his own image and see if it did not resemble him, the stranger lion.

He looked and acknowledged that it did. Then the stranger lion began to roar and asked him to do the same. The lion-sheep tried his voice and was soon roaring as grandly as the other. And he was a sheep no longer. My friends, I would like to tell you all that you are mighty as lions.

Swamiji concludes:

If the room is dark, do you go about beating your chest and crying, "It is dark, dark, dark!" No, the only way to get the light is to strike a light, and then the darkness goes. The only way to realise the light above you is to strike the spiritual light within you, and the darkness of sin and impurity will flee away. Think of your higher self, not of your lower.

*(Complete Works of Swami Vivekananda, Vol.1, Soul, God and Religion, p326-327)

CHAPTER ELEVEN

Selected Quotations

Following are the words uttered by the lips of the Swami Vivekananda. These should inspire and guide you in every moment and challenge. As an exercise, categorize each quote as Concentration (C) Strength (S), Learning (L), Knowledge (K), Development (D), Unselfishness (U) or other for your own reference.

(1) Arise, awake and stop not till the desired end is reached. (CW(3), p318)

(2) The goal of mankind is knowledge. (CW (1), p27)

(3) Strength is life, weakness is death. (CW(5), p352)

(4) True progress is slow but sure. (CW(5), p78)

(5) Each is great in his own place. (CW(7), p7)

(6) You can do anything and everything, you are almighty. (CW(2) p300)

(7) Strength is in goodness, in purity (CW(5), p409)

(8) Every man must develop according to his nature. (CW(5), 292)

(9) Too much of everything is bad. (CW(7), 482)

(10) Never say, "No", never say, "I cannot", for you are infinite. (CW(2) p300)

(11) Never are the wants of a beggar fulfilled. (CW(5), p353)

(12) Anything that changes cannot be immortal. (CW(1), p254)

(13) Do not be in a hurry, do not go out to imitate anybody else. (CW(3), p381)

(14) No one can get anything unless he earns it. This is an eternal law. (CW (1), p31)

(15) What the world wants is character. (CW(7), p501)

(16) Competition rouses envy, and it kills the kindliness of the heart. (CW(1) p71)

(17) Unselfishness is more paying, only people have not the patience to practice it. (CW(1), p32)

(18) Arise, awake, for the time is propitious. Already everything is opening out before us. Be bold and fear not. (CW(3), p318)

(19) Do not say, "You are bad"; say only, "You are good, but be better. (CW(7), p22)

(20) Bold words and bolder deeds are what we want. (CW(7), p501)

(21) There is only one purpose in the whole of life — education. (CW(8), p431)

(22) Man is born to conquer nature and not to follow it. (CW(5), 409)

(23) The power of concentration is the only key to the treasure-house of knowledge. (CW(2), p391)

(24) Education is the manifestation of the perfection already in man. (CW(4), p358)

(25) This world is neither good nor evil; each man manufactures world for himself. (CW(1), p75)

(26) Man is not travelling from error to truth, but from truth to truth from lower truth to higher truth. (CW(1), p17)

(27) The secret of life is not enjoyment but education through experience. (CW(5), p150)

(28) We are lions in sheep's clothing of habit, we are hypnotised into weakness by our surroundings. (CW(8), 257)

(29) We may go on accumulating things for our physical enjoyment, but only what we earn is really ours. (CW(1) p31)

(30) Each soul is potentially divine. The goal is to manifest this Divinity within, by controlling nature, external and internal. (CW(1), p257)

(31) The chaste brain has tremendous energy and gigantic will-power. Without chastity, there can be no spiritual strength. (CW(1), p263)

(32) Liberty is the first condition of growth. (CW(4), p367)

(33) Every man should take up his ideal own ideal and endeavour to accomplish it. That is a surer way to progress than taking up other man's ideal, which he can never hope to accomplish. (CW(1), p41)

(34) This "I and mine" causes the whole misery. With the sense of possession comes selfishness, and selfishness brings on misery. (CW(1), p100)

(35) The goal may be distant, but awake, arise, and stop not till the goal is reached. (CW(2), p87)

(36) Our first duty is not to hate ourselves, because to advance we must have faith in ourselves first and then in God. (CW(1) p38)

(37) Neither money pays, nor name, nor fame, nor learning; it is character that can cleave through adamantine walls of difficulties. (CW(7), p487)

(38) We are what our thoughts have made us; so take care of what you think. Words are secondary. Thoughts live, they travel far. (CW(7), p14)

(39) Work incessantly, but give up all attachment to work." "Misery comes through attachment, not through work. (CW(1) , p100)

(40) No one was ever really taught by another; each of us has to teach himself. The external teacher offers only the suggestion which rouses the internal teacher to work to understand things. (CW(1), p93)

(41) Every soul is a young eagle soaring higher and higher, gathering more and more strength, till it reaches the Glorious Sun. (CW (1), p17)

(42) We only get what we deserve. It is a lie when we say, the world is bad and we are good. It can never be so. It is a terrible lie we tell ourselves. (CW(2), p8)

(43) Ignorance is the mother of all the evil and all the misery we see. Let men have light, let them be pure and spiritually strong and educated, then alone will misery cease in the world, not before. (CW(1), p53)

(44) In the vast majority of cases, it would be found that it was misery that taught more than happiness, it was poverty that taught more than wealth, it was blows that brought out their inner fire more than praise. (CW (1), p27)

(45) Our duty to others means helping others; doing good to the world. Why should we do good to the world? Apparently to help the world, but really to help ourselves. (CW(1), p75)

(46) The eye is in the forehead and not in the back. Move onward and carry into practice that which you are very proud to call your religion, (CW(5), p50)

(47) Books are infinite in number, and time is short; therefore the secret of knowledge is to take what is essential. Take that and try to live up to it. (CW(1), p236)

(48) All that man has to do is to take care of three things: good thought, good word, good deed. That is all. (CW(1), p492)

(49) The powers of the mind are like rays of light dissipated; when they are concentrated, they illumine. This is our only means of knowledge. (CW(1), p129)

(50) All expansion is life, all contraction is death. All love is expansions all selfishness is contraction. (CW(6), p320)

(51) Do not wait for anybody or anything. Do whatever you can. Build your hope on none. (CW(5), p34)

(52) Let us work on, doing as we go whatever happens to be our duty, and being ever ready to put our shoulders to the wheel. Then surely shall we see the Light! (CW(1) p71)

(53) Every mental and physical blow that is given to the soul, by which, as it were, fire is struck from it, and by which its own power and knowledge are discovered, is Karma, this word being used in its widest sense (CW(1), p29) - (50)

(54) The great king Yudhishthira once said that the most wonderful thing in life is that every moment, we see people dying around us, and yet we think we shall never die. Surrounded by fools on every side, we think we are the only exceptions, the only learned men. (CW(1), p246)

(55) The gift of knowledge is a far higher gift than that of food and clothes; it is even higher than giving life to a man, because the real life of man consists of knowledge. Ignorance is death, knowledge is life. Life is of very little value, if it is a life in the dark, groping through ignorance and misery. (CW(1), p52)

(56) Seek the highest, always the highest, for in the Highest is eternal bliss. If I am hunt, I will hunt the lion. (CW(5), p275)

(57) You are infinite, deathless, birthless. Because you are infinite spirit, it does not befit you to be a slave. ... Arise! Awake! Stand up and fight! Die if you must. There is none to help you. You are all the world. (CW(1), p461

(58) Education is not the amount of information that is put into your brain and runs riot there, undigested, all your life. (CW(3), p302)

(59) The apple tree should not be judged by the standard of the oak, nor the oak by that of the apple. To judge the apple tree you must take the apple standard, and for the oak, its own standard. (CW(1), p41)

(60) A fool may buy all the books in the world, and they will be in his library, but he will be able to read only those that he deserves to, and this deserving is produced by Karma." (CW(1), p31)

(61) This is the great fact: strength is life, weakness is death. Strength is felicity, life eternal, immortal; weakness is constant strain and misery: weakness is death. (CW(2), p3)

(62) This world is the great gymnasium where we come to make ourselves strong. CW(5), p410)

(63) The chaste brain has tremendous energy and gigantic will-power. Without chastity there can be no spiritual strength. (CW(1), p263)

(64) We are responsible for what we are; and whatever we wish ourselves to be, we have the power to make ourselves. If what we are now has been the result of our own past actions, it certainly follows that whatever we wish to be in future can be produced by our present actions; so we have to know how to act. (CW(1), p31)

(65) Every mental and physical blow that is given to the soul, by which, as it were, fire is struck from it, and by which its own power and knowledge are discovered, is Karma, this word being used in its widest sense (CW(1), p29)

(66) You are infinite, deathless, birthless. Because you are infinite spirit, it does not befit you to be a slave. ... Arise! Awake! Stand up and fight! Die if you must. There is none to help you. You are all the world. (CW(1), p461

(67) Every soul is a young eagle soaring higher and higher, gathering more and more strength, till it reaches the Glorious Sun. (CW (1), p17)

(68) The ideal of all education, all training, should be this man-making. But, instead of that, we are always trying to polish up the outside. What use in polishing up the outside when there is no inside? The end and aim of all training is to make the man grow. (CW(2), p15)

(69) The weak have no place here, in this life or in any other life. Weakness leads to slavery. Weakness leads to all kinds of misery, physical and mental. (CW(2), p3)

(70) Truth is strengthening. Truth is purity, truth is all-knowledge; truth must be strengthening, must be enlightening, must be invigorating. CW(3), p225

(71) This is the first lesson to learn: be determined not to curse anything outside, not to lay the blame upon anyone outside, but be a man, stand up, lay the blame on yourself. You will find, that is always true. Get hold of yourself. (CW(2) p8)

(72) Help thyself out by thyself. None else can help thee, friend. For thou alone art thy greatest enemy, thou alone art thy greatest friend. Get hold of the Self, then. Stand up. Don't be afraid. (CW(2), p403)

(73) I am sure if you look back upon your lives you will find that you were always vainly trying to get help from others which never came. All the help that has come was from within yourselves. You only had the fruits of what you yourselves worked for, and yet you were strangely hoping all the time for help. (CW(2), p324)

(74) We are everything, ready to do everything, we can do everything, and man must do everything. (CW(3), p376)

(75) If education is identical with information, the libraries are the greatest sages in the world, and encyclopaedias are the Rishis. (CW(3), p302)

(76) The more we learn, the more he find out how ignorant we are, how multiform and multi-sided is this mind of man. (CW(2) p25)

(77) The search for truth is the expression of strength – not the groping of a weak, blind man. (CW(5), 410)

(78) Take the whole responsibility on your own shoulders, and know that you are the creator of your own destiny. All the strength and succour you want is within yourselves. Therefore, make your own future. (CW(2),

p225)

(79) Never mind the struggles, the mistakes. I never heard a cow tell a lie, but it is only a cow — never a man. So never mind these failures, these little backslidings; hold the ideal a thousand times, and if you fail a thousand times, make the attempt once more. (CW(2), p152)

(80) "Brave, bold men, these are what we want. What we want is vigour in the blood, strength in the nerves, iron muscles and nerves of steel, not softening namby-pamby ideas. Avoid all these. Avoid all mystery. (CW (3), p278)

(81) What we want is muscles of iron and nerves of steel. We have wept long enough. No more weeping, but stand on your feet and be men. It is a man-making religion that we want. It is man-making theories that we want. It is man-making education all round that we want. (CW(3), p224)

(82) We must have life-building, man-making, character-making assimilation of ideas. If you have assimilated five ideas and made them your life and character, you have more education than any man who has got by heart a whole library. (CW(3), p302)

(83) All power is within you; you can do anything and everything. Believe in that, do not believe that you are weak; do not believe that you are half-crazy lunatics, as most of us do nowadays. You can do anything and everything without even the guidance of anyone. All power is there. Stand up and express the divinity within you. (CW(3), p284)

(84) Verily, these three are rare to obtain and come only through the grace of God — human birth, desire to obtain Moksha, and the company of the great-souled ones." (CW(3), p451)

(85) If you think yourselves weak, weak you will be; if you think yourselves strong, strong you will be; if you think yourselves impure, impure you will be; if you think yourselves pure, pure you will be. This teaches us not to think ourselves as weak, but as strong, omnipotent, omniscient. (CW(3), p130)

(86) Take care! Beware of everything that is untrue; stick to truth and we shall succeed, maybe slowly, but surely. (CW(4), p370)

(87) Feel, my children, feel; feel for the poor, the ignorant, the downtrodden; feel till the heart stops and the brain reels and you think you will go mad — then pour the soul out at the feet of the Lord, and then will come power, help, and indomitable energy. (CW(4), p367)

(88) By education I do not mean the present system, but something in the line of positive teaching. Mere book learning won't do. We want that education by which character is formed, strength of mind is increased, the intellect is expanded, and by which one can stand on one's own feet. (CW(5), p342)

(89) Anything that makes you weak physically, intellectually, and spiritually, reject as poison; there is no life in it, it cannot be true. CW(3), p225)

(90) Everything can be sacrificed for truth, truth cannot be sacrificed for anything. (CW(5), 410)

(91) You have to grow from inside out. None can teach you, none can make you spiritual. There is no other teacher than your own soul. (CW(5), 410)

(92) What is education? Is it book learning? No. Is it diverse knowledge? Not even that. The training by which the current and expression of will are brought under control and become fruitful is called education. (CW(4), 490)

(93) You cannot teach a child any more than you can grow a plant. All you can do is on the negative side — you can only help. It is a manifestation from within; it develops its own nature — you can only take away obstructions. (CW(5), p410)

(94) My child, what I want is muscles of iron and nerves of steel, inside which dwells a mind of the same material as that of which the thunderbolt is made. Strength, manhood, Kshatra Virya + BrahmaTeja. (CW(5), p117)

(95) Each soul is potentially divine. The goal is to manifest this Divinity within, by controlling nature, external and internal. (CW(1), p257)

(96) Take up one idea. Make that one idea your life — think of it, dream of it, live on that idea. Let the brain, muscles, nerves, every part of your body, be full of that idea, and just leave every other idea alone. This is the way to success, and this is the way great spiritual giants are produced. (CW(1), p177)

(97) The soul is a circle whose circumference is nowhere (limitless), but whose centre is in some body. Death is but a change of centre. (CW(5), p271)

(98) To me, the very essence of education is concentration of mind, not the collecting of facts. (CW(6), p38)

(99) If I had to do my education over again, and had any voice in the matter, I would not study facts at all. I would develop the power of concentration and detachment, and then with a perfect instrument, I could collect facts at will. (CW(6), p38)

(100) I see it clear as daylight that you all have infinite power in you. Rouse that up; arise, arise — apply yourselves heart and soul, gird up your loins. (CW(7), p176)

(101) The highest manifestation of strength is to keep ourselves calm and on our own feet. (CW(5), p279)

After reading the stories and quotations, you would appreciate the profound advice. Contemplate on them and remember them for life. Surely, these will help you to steer through the challenges ahead and express your potential.

Note: The abbreviation CW is for Complete Works of Swami Vivekananda, followed by the volume number, followed by the page number of the book published by Advaita Ashrama. You can look at the source for detailed reading. Complete Works of Swami Vivekananda: https://advaitaashrama.org/cw/

CHAPTER TWELVE

Swamiji's Advice for Work

No one can get anything unless he earns it. This is an eternal law. We may sometimes think it is not so, but in the long run, we become convinced of it.

A man may struggle all his life for riches; he may cheat thousands, but he finds at last that he did not deserve to become rich, and his life becomes a trouble and a nuisance to him.

We may go on accumulating things for our physical enjoyment, but only what we earn is really ours. A fool may buy all the books in the world, and they will be in his library, but he will be able to read only those that he deserves to, and this deserving is produced by Karma.

Our Karma determines what we deserve and what we can assimilate. We are responsible for what we are; and whatever we wish ourselves to be, we have the power to make ourselves.

If what we are now has been the result of our own past actions, it certainly follows that whatever we wish to be in future can be produced by our present actions; so we have to know how to act.

You will say, "What is the use of learning how to work? Everyone works in some way or other in this world." But there is such a thing as frittering away our energies.

With regard to Karma-Yoga, the Gita says that it is doing work with cleverness and as a science; by knowing how to work, one can obtain the greatest results.

You must remember that all work is simply to bring out the power of the mind which is already there, to wake up the soul. The power is inside every man, so is knowing; the different works are like blows to bring them out, to cause these giants to wake up.

....

Swamiji concludes:

Work for work's sake. There are some who are really the salt of the earth in every country and who work for work's sake, who do not care for name, or fame, or even to go to heaven. They work just because good will come of it.

There are others who do good to the poor and help mankind from still higher motives because they believe in doing good and love good. The motive for name and fame seldom brings immediate results, as a rule; they come to us when we are old and have almost done with life.

If a man works without any selfish motive in view, does he not gain anything? Yes, he gains the highest. Unselfishness is more paying, only people have not the patience to practice it. It is more paying from the point of view of health also. Love, truth, and unselfishness are not merely moral figures of speech, but they form our highest ideal, because in them lies such a manifestation of power.

In the first place, a man who can work for five days, or even for five minutes, without any selfish motive whatever, without thinking of future, of heaven, of punishment, or anything of the kind, has in him the capacity to become a powerful moral giant.

If a man works without any selfish motive in view, does he not gain anything? Yes, he gains the highest.

Unselfishness is more paying, only people have not the patience to practice it. It is more paying from the point of view of health also.

Love, truth, and unselfishness are not merely moral figures of speech, but they form our highest ideal, because in them lies such a manifestation of power.

In the first place, a man who can work for five days, or even for five minutes, without any selfish motive whatever, without thinking of future, of heaven, of punishment, or anything of the kind, has in him the capacity to become a powerful moral giant.

It is hard to do it, but in the heart of our hearts we know its value, and the good it brings. It is the greatest manifestation of power — this tremendous restraint; self-restraint is a manifestation of greater power than all outgoing action.

A carriage with four horses may rush down a hill unrestrained, or the coachman may curb the horses. Which is the greater manifestation of power, to let them go or to hold them?

*(Complete Works of Swami Vivekananda, Vol.1, Karma Yoga, Chapter 1, p31-32)

Swami Vivekananda

Eternal messages:
"Help and not Fight",
"Assimilation and not Destruction",
"Harmony and Peace and not Dissension."

CHAPTER THIRTEEN

Duties

This chapter presents key lessons in the words of Swami Vivekananda from his lecture titled Each Is Great In His Own Place. Here, you will find a set of guidelines for life.

(1) Our first duty is not to hate ourselves.

(2) A man must be active in order to pass through activity to perfect calmness.

(3) Inactivity should be avoided by all means. Activity always means resistance.

Duty for the self and others

(4) Each is great in his own place, but the duty of the one is not the duty of the other.

(5) Every man should take up his own ideal and endeavour to accomplish it.

(6) Let every one do the best he can for realising his own ideal.

(7) Our duty is to encourage every one in his struggle to live up to his own highest ideal and strive at the same time to make the ideal as near as possible to the truth.

Duties of a householder

(8) The householder should be devoted to God; the knowledge of God should be his goal of life. Yet he must work constantly, perform all his duties; he must give up the fruits of his actions to God.

(9) Knowing that mother and father are the visible representatives of God, [students and] the householder, always and by all means, must please them. If the mother is pleased, and the father, God is pleased with the man. That child is really a good child who never speaks harsh words to his parents.

(10) Before parents one must not utter jokes, must not show restlessness, must not show anger or temper. Before mother or father, a

child must bow down low, and stand up in their presence, and must not take a seat until they order him to sit.

(11) If the householder has food and drink and clothes without first seeing that his mother and his father, his children, his wife, and the poor, are supplied, he is committing a sin. The mother and the father are the causes of this body; so a man must undergo a thousand troubles in order to do good to them.

(12) Before women he must not talk improper language, and never brag of his powers. He must not say, "I have done this, and I have done that."

Duties towards children

(13) A son should be lovingly reared up to his fourth year; he should be educated till he is sixteen. When he is twenty years of age he should be employed in some work; he should then be treated affectionately by his father as his equal.

(14) Exactly in the same manner the daughter should be brought up, and should be educated with the greatest care. And when she marries, the father ought to give her jewels and wealth.

Duties towards brothers and sisters

(15) Then the duty of the man is towards his brothers and sisters, and towards the children of his brothers and sisters, if they are poor, and towards his other relatives, his friends and his servants. Then his duties are towards the people of the same village, and the poor, and anyone that comes to him for help. Having sufficient means, if the householder does not take care to give to his relatives and to the poor, know him to be only a brute; he is not a human being.

(16) Excessive attachment to food, clothes, and the tending of the body, and dressing of the hair should be avoided. The householder must be pure in heart and clean in body, always active and always ready for work.

Duties towards enemies

(17) To his enemies the householder must be a hero. Them he must resist. That is the duty of the householder. He must not sit down in a corner and weep, and talk nonsense about non-resistance. If he does not show himself a hero to his enemies he has not done his duty. And to his friends and relatives, he must be as gentle as a lamb.

Duties while talking

(18) It is the duty of the householder not to pay reverence to the wicked.

(19) Three things he must not talk of. He must not talk in public of his own fame; he must not preach his own name or his own powers; he must not talk of his wealth, or of anything that has been told to him privately.

(20) A man must not say he is poor, or that he is wealthy — he must not brag of his wealth. Let him keep his own counsel; this is his religious duty. This is not mere worldly wisdom; if a man does not do so, he may be held to be immoral.

Going after wealth

(21) He must struggle to acquire a good name by all means. He must not gamble, he must not move in the company of the wicked, he must not tell lies, and must not be the cause of trouble to others.

(22) The householder must speak the truth, and speak gently, using words which people like, which will do good to others; nor should he talk of the business of other men.

(23) A man must go about his duties without taking notice of the sneers and the ridicule of the world.

❧❧❧

Reference: *Each Is Great In His Own Place, Karma Yoga, Chapter II, (CW1).*

Swami Vivekananda

CHAPTER FOURTEEN

ON THE SEA'S BOSOM

In blue sky floats a multitude of clouds —
White, black, of snaky shades and thicknesses;
An orange sun, about to say farewell,
Touches the massed cloud-shapes with streaks of red.

-

The wind blows as it lists, a hurricane
Now carving shapes, now breaking them apart:
Fancies, colours, forms, inert creations —
A myriad scenes, though real, yet fantastic.

.

There light clouds spread, heaping up spun cotton;
See next a huge snake, then a strong lion;
Again, behold a couple locked in love.
All vanish, at last, in the vapoury sky.

.

Below, the sea sings a varied music,
But not grand, O India, nor ennobling:
Thy waters, widely praised, murmur serene
In soothing cadence, without a harsh roar.
*(A poem in Bengali during his return from his second trip
to the West.)* (CW(6), Writings: Prose and Poems)

Other Publications

Stimulating Messages of Swami Vivekananda in English and Bengali

Upcoming

Blockly Games for Computational Thinking for young learners